HOW TO MOVE HOUSE STRESS FREE

THE STEP BY STEP GUIDE TO MOVING HOME SUCCESSFULLY

PETER BLACK

FREE PRINTABLE PDF TO HELP YOU CHOOSE THE RIGHT HOME!

At the back of the book is an opportunity to join the Peter Black mailing list.

As a reward for signing up to the mailing list, you will receive a free printable pdf of the property scorecard covered in this book, that you can use to help you feel more confident that you are making the right choice for your next home.

.

ACKNOWLEDGMENTS

For L and N, my moving buddies...

INTRODUCTION

Who on Earth enjoys moving? I don't mean the idea of choosing a new home, enjoying more space, and the new lease of life that a new home might offer. All of these things can be lovely, exciting, and, at times, hugely relieving. I mean the actual nuts and bolts of dealing with indifferent estate agents, chasing up lethargic solicitors, worrying about who is going to look after the cat while you move, and trying to keep your own sanity when it feels like the carpet can be ripped out from underneath your feet at any moment? I would venture that not many people like this process, and that actually most people HATE the idea of moving. It's not hard to see why.

Moving is normally a horribly stressful and anxious time.

Almost two-thirds of the 2,000 people surveyed, who had moved in the previous three years, highlighted the process as the most stressful thing that they had experienced during that time. It beat other difficult processes such as a relationship breakdown, a divorce, and starting a new job. About 42% of the same group suggested that moving was the most stressful thing they had ever experienced in their lives! In some ways, it is hard to believe that moving has been identified as the most stressful thing in lives that might include bereavement, redundancy, or the ending of significant and meaningful relationships. However, this is the truth of it. An average Briton will move five times in their lives, and the stress of it can remain present for up to three months after the move has been completed. If we are not careful, the process of moving can be as unpleasant as it is reinvigorating, and the associated stress can be problematic. The stress can leave us tearing our hair out, at the throats of our loved ones, and can take any semblance of enjoyment and pleasure out of a process that has the potential to be quite exciting and gratifying.

The good news is that moving does not have to the stressful experience described above.

This is where this book comes in. In this book, I'm going to show you how to manage the process from start to finish, in a way that helps to keep your decision-making logical, calm, and focused. This book will teach you how to manage the various characters and personalities involved in your move (such as solicitors and estate agents), as well as ensuring that you know why you are making the choices you are, and leaving you in a position where you can be confident about them. This book will also teach you how to stay in control of the whole process, so that you feel empowered rather than helpless, and it will help you work towards maintaining a sense of genuine serenity, as opposed to stressed out confusion. This book will teach you how to take care of your own wellbeing, so that you can actually enjoy your move, rather than viewing and experiencing it as a number of agonising steps that appear to be deliberately designed to tip you over the edge. It is a concise, clearly written, and easy-to-understand guide to managing your move in a stress free and psychologically informed way.

Why should you listen to me? That's a fair question. I have bought and sold property in the past, meaning I have first-hand experience of the process. More importantly, I have a wealth of experience and knowledge in my work as a psychologist, meaning that the tips and hacks I will provide you in this book have been tried and tested, and have already helped others in managing their home moves which hugely reduced levels of stress. The information included in this book has had such a positive impact on those home movers I have shared it with that I feel compelled to share it with everyone.

I promise you that if you follow the information and guidance available in this book, you will experience a different type of move. You will feel more in control of the process, happier and more content with your decisions, and you will second-guess yourself less. You will also be much more vigilant to your own wellbeing and happiness throughout the experience of moving. I cannot promise you that the move will not include any setbacks, knocks, or points of pressure, and I would be lying if I said I could offer that. I am not a shaman or a hypnotist. What I can offer you is a set of tried and tested techniques that are bound to improve your moving experience.

Do not take your emotional wellbeing for granted. In this book is an opportunity to make the process easier and less painful. Life is stressful enough and, if you are planning to move soon, you are likely to know that you are on the cusp of what can be a difficult, tense, nerve-wracking, and emotionally charged long-term activity. Reading the information in this book is one simple thing you can do to greatly and quickly reduce the amount of stress you are vulnerable to during the moving process. It is a step-by-step guide to looking after yourself, your move, and the loved ones in your life making the move with you (including the cat). The book also includes an important element often ignored by other books on the subject. It gives you strategies and step-by-step guides to follow, so that you can feel confident that the choices you are making are right for you and your loved ones. Nobody wants to regret a home move, and this book will help to greatly reduce the chances of that happening.

The information and guidance in this book you are about to read has been proven to contribute to a more serene moving process. All you have to do to achieve this is read the information in this book, and each chapter will provide you with more insight into how to make your move smoother, and it will leave you feeling more able to control decisions and how the move progresses.

So, what are you waiting for? Let's get you moving ....

HOW TO USE THIS BOOK

Congratulations! If you've made it this far, it means that you are on the road to making your move less stressful, easier to manage, and a more all-round, more positive experience! That's assuming you bought the book for yourself of course. You may be a very kind-hearted person who, in fact, has bought this book for a friend, colleague, or family member who is about to embark on what can be quite a tricky journey. You may feel that you know a bit about what's ahead, or you may be a complete novice to this moving game, looking to purchase your first home. Whatever the reason you've decided to read this book, and however it ended up in front of you, I expect you would like to know what's in store in the rest of the book.

This book has five main parts, which are briefly outlined below.

Part one of the book is focused on helping you to feel confident and confirm in your own mind that you do want (or need) to leave your current home. This might seem like a no-brainer; otherwise, you wouldn't have picked up this book, right? Well, this first part of the book helps to set the foundation for your move. There is nothing worse than working through the process of moving and not actually being sure that you are doing the right thing. If you have gone through a clear process and arrived at the conclusion that it is time for you to move on, then you can feel comfortable and content moving forward, without the presence of nagging doubts holding you back.

Part two of the book helps you to identify two important factors. What are the goals and expectations of your move? If you can be certain that you know what you want your next home to include, how you want it to look, what features you feel you need, and more importantly I expect, how you want your next home to *feel,* this sets the tone for a more productive move. We will cover this more later, and I'm not sure I know how to explain it, but there were plenty of times my wife and I would return from looking at a house, and confirm that whilst the property had the physical characteristics we were looking for, it just didn't quite *feel* right. This part of the book will also force you to be realistic with yourselves—what can you afford and what does that mean for the kind of home you should be looking at and considering? This part will mean that you and the rest of your moving party (those who will be living with you in the new home) are on the same page about what you are looking for.

Part three of the book is interested in managing the move, from a psychological perspective. This involves planning the sequencing of activities—should you look at houses before you have sold yours, or should you wait? This will depend on your personality and thinking patterns. Also covered in this part are practical tips on how to manage your relationships with estate agents and solicitors, potentially awkward interactions that can be causes of stress in themselves. You will also learn 'how' to view houses in a productive way that keeps you grounded and focused on your home moving goals. This part of the book considers the best strategies to make and receive offers for properties; this can often feel like a game of chess. so I will ensure you have the inside track on how to negotiate strongly and confidently.

Part four of the book is focused on the actual moving process. Again, there will be some practical tips and suggestions, but, actually, most of the chapter will talk about how to cope with a transition whilst maintaining and protecting your psychological wellbeing. It includes tips about how to declutter and how to get through moving day without falling out with any of your nearest and dearest.

Section five of the book talks about how to manage your wellbeing throughout the whole process. It is packed full of tips and things to bear in mind whilst engaged in this overall process. It will help you to manage the long delays and waits, the confusing silences and poor communication that seem to plague house moves at times. It will also encourage you to not forget the rest of your life during the move, as moving can become an all-encompassing and life dominating event.

So, that's what you can expect from this book. It is designed to act as a guidebook for getting through the process of moving and retaining your emotional and psychological wellbeing. Stress can be hugely damaging to our health, so we should take every opportunity to meaningfully prepare for stressful parts of our lives when we can foresee them. When experiencing a sudden bereavement or a relationship deterioration, we cannot always plan to manage our wellbeing. I guess the same could also be said for home moving—we may suddenly be made homeless for a number of reasons. However, for the most part, we move because we want to, and therefore we can prepare in advance to get through the process in a healthy and psychologically 'safe' way.

What this book is not, however, is a hugely detailed step-by-step guide on how to manage the practicalities of a home move. I'm not going to explain in detail how mortgages work (although I will mention them), nor am I going to get stuck into land laws or the various processes involved in buying and selling a home. I'm sorry if that's what you were hoping for here, but there are plenty of books on topics such as these. And, of course, that is not to say that if you ended up here through serendipity, that there are still not lots of useful information you can gain by reading on anyway.

Whatever the reason for you reading this, it's lovely to have you!

How you use this book is, of course, totally up to you. You may choose to read it cover to cover, or you may just decide that only certain chapters will apply to your circumstances, and so you may just choose to read those. Either way, I am very confident you will take something useful away from your experience with this book. My advice is that you read it all, but then I would say that! On a serious note, I would suggest that you do not skip part one of the book—this part is the foundation for the rest of the book, and will leave you content with the decision to move that you have may have already arrived at.

SECTION I:

DECIDING TO LEAVE YOUR HOME

Chapters 1 – 2

1

WHY DO YOU WANT TO MOVE?

In this chapter, we'll spend some time thinking about the rationale for your move. Why is it that you think a move is right for you at this point in your life? Our homes are hugely central to our lives, and often we consider these places to be sacred, our sanctuary from the chaos and madness that our lives can include. However, our homes can also be the source of less pleasant emotions. If our home does not provide us with sanctuary from the stress of life in general, then we may be left thinking that it is time for a new home. Because our homes can trigger so many emotions in us, they can also lead, if we are not careful, to some rash decision-making when it comes to where we live. This can include a decision to move. Below are a number of reasons that people may choose to move, and it is highly likely that you will spot your most compelling reason for moving in this list somewhere. As you read through the list, try to think about the 'problem' your current home presents for you.

- My relationship status is changing

Relationships start and end, this is a fact of life. It may be the case that, sadly, a co-habiting relationship has ended, and it is not healthy for you to continue living with your former partner. Alternatively, it might be that you are involved in a relationship that is progressing well, and that you are both at the point where you would like to commence co-habiting with each other. Changes to a relationship status are a very common reason people move, and it can be positive whether they mark the beginning or end of a relationship.

- I'm not on the property ladder

Renting can feel like a real drag. There is nothing more frustrating than feeling like you're lining somebody else's pocket and adding to their wealth, while you tread water paying a monthly rent that is often not that far off the amount you would pay for a mortgage anyway. Buying your own first home is an excellent reason to move, and it can be an incredibly exciting experience. In 2017, there were 359,000 first-time-buying households, and this goes to show that people are still extremely keen to own their own bricks and mortar.

- I'm being kicked out of my home

A sad reality of life is that sometimes people are evicted from their homes. This can cause a huge amount of stress, but evictions are commonplace in our world today. Being evicted is very rarely a choice, and usually follows some financial difficulty. However, being subjected to an eviction does not mean that you should always have an eye on your next home. Clearly, you may have less choice than others have if you are struggling financially, but it may be that your next home is not ideal and should only be a short-term fix.

- My life is boring, and I want a change

Sometimes in life, we just feel like we need a change. You may feel that moving is a good way of blowing away the cobwebs, or just shaking up a life that may have started to feel a bit repetitive or dull. Moving can freshen things up, especially if you are moving to a different part of the country, or maybe even to a different country completely. However, it is a reason to be wary of. As will be covered in more detail in the next chapter, you will need to be careful that a move for this reason is not simply papering over the cracks, and that whatever you are trying to move away or escape from, does not simply come with you.

- I am going to be changing jobs and live too far away

It is quite often the case that people need to move in order to progress in their careers. As people often study or train for many years in order to access a certain career or job role, they are often prepared for a significant geographical move at some point in the future. Commuting can be a real hindrance for your work/life balance, and a well-planned and logistical home move can be incredibly helpful to avoid the nuisance that a commute can provide in life.

- I'm getting older, and my home is no longer suitable

We are all going to get older; this is unavoidable. As we age, we're going to have different types of needs for many parts of our lives, and this, of course, will include our homes. We may have mobility challenges that mean that we do not want to have to try to deal with stairs, or we may no longer have the ability to manage a large garden and may not want to pay someone else to do this for us. These kind of age-related life changes can result in us concluding that it is time for a home move.

- My home is too big, or I cannot afford it anymore

Most people want a home that is suitable for the number of people who live in it and one that has everything they think they need. Things in life change, and this can often lead to a review of housing requirements. If your children have flown the nest, and you have no plans for a study or home gym, you might be considering cashing in on your home, downsizing, and finally being mortgage free. You might want the extra money to go and explore the world, or perhaps start working part time instead of full time. Downsizing can be a great reason for moving.

- I need more space, or I want a better-quality home

This could be considered the opposite to downsizing! It might be that you are in a position to buy a bigger home, as you have started to earn more money. It might be that you are starting a family and would like some outside space that you do not currently have. It might even be that you just want more space, even if you don't have any desire to fill it with children! Upgrading and upsizing is a great reason to move, and it can really bring some extra enjoyment and comfort to your lives.

- I don't like the area I live in

This is one of those situations where beauty is in the eye of the beholder. A reality of life is that we all have preferences about where we live, and we will all have positive and negative views about our local areas and the districts with them. It might be that you are struggling with the neighbours, or you prefer the schools in a different area. Ultimately, we will all have our own ideas about what constitutes a 'nice' area, but I think it is fair to say that if we have the opportunity to move to a 'nicer' area, and can achieve it, most of us probably would.

Above is a list of reasons why people may decide to try to leave their homes for a new one. The list is not exhaustive, and whilst it is likely that your reason (or a variation of the reason) is on that list somewhere, there is a chance that it is not. This chapter is interested in helping you determine which 'problem' you feel your current home presents you with in your life. The next chapter is going to encourage you to consider, in an objective way, the wisdom of moving in an effort to address that problem.

2
_____

DO YOU ACTUALLY NEED TO MOVE?

In the last chapter, we covered some of the reasons that people may decide to leave their homes, and some of the problems that people may feel their current home causes them, or at least the way in which their current home make their lives less comfortable than they would like them to be. I expect that you found your reason or 'problem' on that list, or at least a variation of your problem.

This chapter is going to move things on a little and help you make sense of whether a home move is actually going to 'solve' the problem you feel is being caused by your current living circumstances. If you engage in the thinking and exercises presented in this chapter, and still arrive at the end of it convinced that a move is the right thing for you, then you can move forward content that you have thought through what can be a very complex decision, and you can start to think about what you want your next home to look like. Conversely, you may arrive at the conclusion that a move is not the right thing for you at the moment. Either way, you can be content that you have thought this incredibly important decision through thoroughly.

So, how do we conclude if a move is the right thing either way? There are two elements to this. Firstly, we need to establish the potential costs and benefits to you moving your home at this point in your life, and we can do this using a straightforward cost/benefit analysis. Secondly, we need to spend some time thinking about whether a move is actually going to 'solve' the problem you feel your current home is causing you.

The Cost/Benefit Analysis

This is a tool that is very helpful in assisting you to analyse a potential decision, taking into account the potential positive and negative aspects of the decision. It also encourages you to consider both the short-term consequences and the longer-term impacts of the decision. Below is the cost/benefit analysis I produced with my wife before we decided to sell our flat and buy a house.

	Positive	Negative
Short term	-Get away from horrible neighbours -Feel happier -Have some outside space -Less stress -Could have a dishwasher	-A lot of hassle -Possible stress -Expensive
Long term	-Have more space -Build wealth (investment) -Room for more children -Feel more relaxed and happy -Move to a repayment mortgage	-Less disposable income -Possibly expensive renovations

As you can see, for us the cost/benefit analysis was quite clear in suggesting that the move was, overall, likely to be a positive thing for us to do. We knew this because there are more points in the positive column then there are in the negative column. Numbers don't tell the whole story, though. If there is only one item in the negative column, and this is the fact that you almost certainly cannot afford it and will lose a new home within six months, then you might place much more weight on this single point.

The analysis you complete is likely to have some similarities and some differences to our list (not everyone is likely to be as excited about a dishwasher as I was—more about that later). The tool can be really helpful as it gets you thinking about both the good and the bad aspects of the idea of moving, and sometimes (especially if we have already half made our minds up), we don't always spend time thinking about the bits of the idea that disagree with our preliminary decision.

I need to insert a bit of a disclaimer here. The cost/benefit analysis is not a crystal ball, and whilst you may be surprised about some of the things you end up adding to your list, it cannot predict everything that might be relevant to you, your lives, and your potential move. What it will do, is get you thinking about the short-term and long-term consequences in a structured way, and it only has to take about five minutes! Having said this, I would advise grabbing a cup of tea and putting aside half an hour with whoever else the move involves and spending time working through the exercise together. Two heads are certainly better than one, and others (including, possibly, people playing 'devil's advocate') can be of great benefit at this point in your decision-making.

Is moving likely to solve your problem?

Once you have completed your cost/benefit analysis, you will have a firmer sense of whether the idea of moving is a good one in principle. Once you have established this, you can move on to start considering the second important element—is moving actually going to solve the problem you feel your current home is presenting you with?

If your problem is that you don't like the area you live in, are you going to be able to move away or are the surrounding areas likely to be too expensive for you to live in? If you want more space as you are planning to have a child, or to have more children, is it essential that you move to accommodate this? Could changes be made to your current home as an alternative?

If you need to downsize, is doing so likely to make you unhappy? There is a line of argument that just because you do not strictly need all of the rooms in your house you *have* to downsize. If you can afford it, and downsizing would make you less happy, then don't do it. Does moving solve one problem but cause another? It's all well and good moving to have outside space, but if you have no time to enjoy it and the garden becomes an unwieldy source of stress, are you actually in a better situation?

There is no hard and fast way of doing this part of the process. It involves a very honest conversation with yourself and the other people the move is going to affect. In summary, you need to be able to meaningfully and honestly answer the following questions:

• What 'problem' is my current home causing?

• Is moving a good idea in principle? (use your cost/benefit analysis)

• Does moving solve the 'problem' being caused by my current home?

• Will moving cause any new insurmountable problems in my life?

. . .

If you can answer the above questions in a genuine and meaningful way, and feel comfortable with your responses, then you are in a position to conclude whether you should seek to move or not.

This, for the time being, may be the end of the road for your current moving plans. You may have realised that, for whatever reason, now is not the right time. However, you may have concluded that now is the right time for you to move, and you can move forward with the rest of this book feeling content and confident in your position.

Now, we need to get a sense of what your new home needs to provide you with ....

SECTION II:

GOALS AND EXPECTATIONS SETTING

Chapters 3 – 6

3

SHOW ME THE MONEY!

The second part of this book is focused on setting expectations in terms of your next home, and trying to establish what are possible and realistic future homes for you and your loved ones. In this chapter specifically, we'll move on and start to think about your finances. How much can you afford to spend on a new home (through monthly rental or mortgage payments)?

In this chapter, we will consider how much money is likely to be enough to move, and the things you will need to bear in mind when you are thinking about moving. Based on a financial evaluation, by the end of this chapter, you should have a good idea how realistic the proposition of moving actually is. Also covered is what you might choose to do if you conclude that moving is not a financially viable option at this point in your life.

So, why is there a whole chapter devoted to money? Well, put simply, moving is an expensive business. Both ways of living (i.e. buying or renting), to differing degrees, attract moving costs. If you are hoping to buy a house, then you will need to find money for a deposit, the solicitors and estate agent fees, as well as the costs attached to actually moving your possessions and furniture into your new home. If you are planning to move into rented accommodations, then you will often be required to part with a deposit which is held by a third party and then returned (minus any necessary repairs) at the point you vacate the property, as well as a month's rent up front. You then, of course, may have extra moving costs, and there are often unanticipated fees and bills that seem to crop up out of nowhere. It is for reasons like these that we are spending some time thinking about your financial capabilities at this point in time, before we actually launch into looking at potential homes.

As established above, moving can be an expensive process. The estimated cost of moving in 2018 in the UK was £8,885.66. This figure is based on the average UK property price in 2018, and it includes all the necessary fees you will need to pay should you be selling and buying a property. So, this is the figure to bear in in mind. Can you spare this as well as any necessary deposit, as well as the monthly 'running costs' of your new home, such as utility bills and mortgage payments?

Moving from one rental property to another might cost up to £3000 with holding deposits, upfront rent costs, and administration fees. So, whilst this is obviously a cheaper option, it is still a lot of money to find. I'm not trying to be a naysayer or doom merchant here, but I am encouraging you to really establish whether you can afford a move. What I would hate is for you to find the money to get through the move, only to find yourself unable to live in any degree of comfort in your new home because of all of the fees and attached costs that you may have overlooked prior to actually moving.

The figures mentioned above are just rough guides, really, and certainly should not be considered to be financial advice! There are a number of sources of meaningful and more accurate financial guidance. For example, on the Internet there are many *mortgage calculators* that can give you a sense of how much you might be able to borrow, what deposit you will probably need, as well as what you might need to expect to pay in terms of bills and utilities in a bigger home, etc. A word of warning here, a lot of the mortgage calculators available on the Internet are connected to specific banks and financial organisations, so they may only really be telling you what *they* might be willing to lend you. Whilst that information is helpful, and there are probably industry standard rules of thumb (e.g. two and a half times the buyers' income), it is probably wise to search for a calculator that is objective and not connected to a specific bank or building society.

Probably, the best thing you can do is talk to a financial advisor. This service should be free, as they often work on a commission basis, which means they charge any lender they are able to connect you with, rather than you needing to pay for their time or services. They are often very well informed about the latest legislation and industry rules, and, in my experience, they are excellent at generating options and offering alternative solutions and ways of buying property and maximising the impact of your money. The only caveat I would add here is that, ultimately, they want to get paid, so they may be keen for you to use their services after your initial consultation. I've never had a hard sell experience with a financial advisor, but just be aware of, and assertive about, what you are comfortable exploring further. Do not allow their enthusiasm or keenness to secure you a mortgage put you in a position where you buy or agree to rent a home you cannot actually afford beyond the mortgage/deposit!

Having done all of the necessary research and digging outlined above, it is time to ask yourself the big question. You may have established that you want to move, and you may be confident that it will help to solve whatever 'problem' you feel your current home presents you with. You need to be really honest and objective when you answer the next question ....

Can you actually and realistically afford to move at this point in time?

If you cannot afford to achieve what you really want to currently, what alternatives are there? Do you have a Plan B? It might be that you move into cheaper accommodations to free up cash to save for a deposit, or it might be that you need to deal with some debt before you can think about moving on. You may not be able to achieve the ideal move you had in mind yet, but you should be able to identify a positive way forward that will move you closer to your goal. This might be a good time to seek advice about debts, or perhaps ask a kind family member if they are able to accommodate you while you save to make your ideal move possible.

In summary, moving, whether that is with the intention of buying a new home or renting a different property, can be an expensive process. If you've reached this point in the chapter, you should have a better sense of whether you can afford such an expense, and, if so, what kinds of costs you might expect to accrue. Of course, it is worth bearing in mind that these pre-move calculations rarely provide the 'whole story,' and there are almost always hidden costs which can derail moves if you are not prepared for them. By now, you know you want to move, and, hopefully, you will be aware of if you can actually afford to move or not.

If you are keen and able to move, then let's turn our attention to starting to think about what your new home is going to need to include ....

4

BUYING VS RENTING

In this chapter, we will focus on a very important topic, should you be renting your next home, or should you be looking to buy your next home. Like lots of things in life, money is going to be the biggest deciding factor here. There are a number of government schemes that are designed to help first-time buyers, but if none of those apply to you, then you are going to need to find a deposit before you can start making offers for houses. Without a deposit, it is very unlikely that you are going to be in a position to consider buying a home.

You might already be a homeowner, in which case your deposit is most likely to be coming from the sale of your current home. You might have been able to save for a deposit over a number of years, had a recent inheritance, or been lucky enough to have a windfall come into your life a different way. This means that you are in the fortunate position of being able to make a choice about buying or renting, and which one you may prefer.

Buying and renting homes both have positive and negative aspects. Sometimes, it can be hard to decide which is the right way forward, so this chapter is written with a view to helping you with this decision. As with all of the chapters of this book, it cannot tell you the right answer, or indeed answer the question for you, but it will enable you to think about the issues that this decision may raise for you. By the end of the chapter, you should be much better placed to finalise this important decision, and then you can be confident that you have considered some of the key issues that are involved in this choice.

One truth is inescapable. You will have to either rent or buy a home. This is an important decision as making the wrong choice can really add to the stress of your life, as if it were not stressful enough already! Imagine deciding to take the plunge and buy, but not actually being able to really afford it in a sustainable way. The extra pressure and stress attached to trying to make mortgage payments is likely to be hugely damaging. This is why you need to be confident that you have made the right choice before you get too far down your moving journey. If you would like to buy but cannot really afford it at the moment, wait. Save up some more money and move at a later point, in a way that is sustainable in the long run. Otherwise, any enjoyment in your new home could quite quickly turn to resentment and stress. Struggle and stress do not make for a happy and relaxed home environment.

Let's start then by having a closer look at the good and bad points of home ownership. Here in the UK, there seems to be an almost pathological obsession with the virtues of owning one's own home, such as having something to pass down to future generations in the family, and people seem to unquestioningly view it as a positive thing, often describing renting as simply 'making someone else richer.' There are grains of truth in some of these beliefs, but the issue is much broader than these points alone.

So, what are the arguments for home ownership then? Well, one clear benefit is that when you have finished paying off the mortgage, that house belongs to you. This means that you get to totally eliminate the biggest living expense you are likely to have. Of course, there are always going to be bills to pay and things like council tax, but you will stop having what is likely to be your biggest monthly expenditure. Hopefully, over the course of repaying your mortgage, your house has increased in value meaning that it will be worth more than you bought it for, and who doesn't love a profit!

Obviously, depending on things such as interest rates and other related issues, it can be cheaper to pay a mortgage than it is to rent. I can speak from personal experience on this point. Before we moved into our current home, we were living in a flat that we had a mortgage on. Because of the very low interest rates, we were at one point, for over a year, paying £189 a month for our mortgage! If we were renting the same flat we could have expected to pay anywhere between £550 and £600 a month.

If you own your own home, you are pretty much able to do whatever you want with it (within local planning rules of course). This could mean that you could add an extension to your home, convert the loft into living space, or even something as simple as being free to decorate your home to your own tastes, without the need for permission from others. If there are problems within the property, resolving them is much more within your control, and you do not have to wait around for a potentially disinterested landlord to step in and resolve the issue.

If you are a first-time buyer, there are a lot of learning opportunities to be had from home ownership. There's the obvious experience you'll gain for next time you buy and sell in the housing market, and it's a great way to kick-start some significant financial planning. This is a skill that is so important when you are running a household, and you will learn skills such as budgeting quickly (if you do not already have those skills). A possible benefit of buying a property is that you may be more likely to stay settled in one place. This means that there is an increased chance you will become part of the local community, which can lead to making lifelong friends.

So, what about renting instead of buying? Let's deal with the idea that it is a waste of money. It's not. If you rent, you are exchanging money for somewhere to live. This is not a waste of money, and, indeed, you would not be able to say the same about buying food, yet the two principles are the same. You are exchanging money for a service you need (i.e. food and shelter). The idea that renting is a waste of money is something of a red herring in my view. I think what people actually mean when they say this is that renting is adding so someone else's wealth, rather than your own. But, if you view your home as somewhere to live and shelter for you and your loved ones, then the wealth attached to that becomes less important.

Whilst I think it is fair to say that most people like to be settled in one place for as long as it suits them, it would be wrong to conclude that this is true of everyone. Some people enjoy a more nomadic lifestyle, and renting rather than buying means that you are much more able to move from place to place, exploring other parts of the area, country, or even continent! Most rental agreements last six months, meaning that you are free to move on at the end of that agreement, if this is what you want to do.

If you rent, you do not need to worry about house prices. Investing in a home is a huge financial commitment, and one that means once you have done this you can become twitchy every time you hear or read about the housing market. Part of the anxiety for homeowners is the dreaded negative equity (where the value of your home drops below what you paid for it), as this can effectively make it impossible for you to sell your home, as you will not recoup enough money to repay the mortgage, or you could eat up your deposit because of the gap between the market value and your mortgage debt.

If you rent, you will not be responsible for the costs attached to maintaining the building. If the boiler suddenly gives up, it is the landlord who is responsible for getting it repaired and paying for it. Also, renting tends to need less cash up front. Whilst you would probably need a deposit of thousands of pounds to buy, in order to rent you often only need six to eight weeks' worth of rent upfront to cover the deposit and first month of rent.

All of the above points are valid to differing degrees, and my wife and I considered them in our own decision, too. There are always individual factors that will impact on what choice is right for you, and so much depends on the individual factors that apply to your situation. For some people, buying a house will be a bad financial decision, but for others, it will not be. As long as you have thought it through and have arrived at a decision that feels right for you and your circumstances, then you can move forward with conviction and confidence.

Here is a very simple set of questions to ask yourself to help determine if you are ready to buy a home:

1. Do you have savings worth at least 10% of the property value you are looking to buy?

YES – Go to question 2.

NO – You are probably going to be unable to buy now unless you go through a government scheme, or have quick access to the money through other means (family gift/inheritance).

. . .

2. Have you enough cash to cover stamp duty, legal fees, furniture, and repairs?

YES – Go question 3.

NO – It would be wise to keep renting until you can afford the extra costs of buying.

3. Are you happy to settle down in a house for at least several years?

YES – Go to question 4.

NO – If you're looking for the flexibility to move quickly, you are better off renting.

4. Are you happy to decorate, repair, and renovate?

YES – You should consider buying!

NO – You may be better off renting and leave all the household repairs to your landlord.

In summary, no one can really tell you if you should be buying or renting. This is a personal decision that is dependent on a number of circumstances, most of which would have been included above. You will need to think this part of the process through very thoroughly, and there will need to be an honest and robust examination of your current financial position. However, having considered the above, you should be feeling much more confident about the final decision you arrive at, whether that is to rent or buy your next home.

5

WHAT DO YOU WANT IN YOUR NEW HOME?

If you're still reading now, that means you have already made a number of key decisions in your home moving journey. You've decided that your current home presents you with a problem that leaves you feeling dissatisfied for some reason(s). You've concluded that factually and objectively, you are in a financial position to move, and that this will actually address the problem(s) you are unhappy with. These should also feel like quite rational and logical decisions.

If you've followed the steps in this book so far, you can trust those feelings, knowing that you have done your best to really think through your options and choices, and you should feel safe in the knowledge that you are not rushing into anything on an impulsive whim! If you are reading this thinking, 'I'm not convinced I should have got this far,' then go back, re-read, and work through the exercises, perhaps with an objective friend who has no personal investment in your moving decision. It's not too late—you're not committed, and nothing is more distressing then realising later in the process that now is not the right time to move, or that you are not moving for the right reasons.

Still here? Okay then, we can move on. This chapter is going to look at a very simple exercise that will help you start to identify the types of features and characteristics you would like your new home to have. Do you want/need a garden? How many bedrooms do you think you need? This is the part where you get to just freewheel and throw ideas around. To do this, we're going to use a tool that you may have heard of before, called 'brainstorming.'

At this point in the process, we are only interested in getting down as many ideas as possible, and that's why brainstorming is a great tool to use at this time. Brainstorming is possible alone, but it does tend to work better in groups. Normally, moves involve more than one person, so perhaps think about getting others who will also be living in your new home involved (i.e. this might include children or just your partner). The goal is the spontaneous generation of ideas—what do the people involved really want from their new home. There will be some things that might seem obvious (ideally, everyone would have somewhere to sleep)! But, what about the location, what kinds of things should be considered there—proximity to schools, or perhaps the family would like to be nearer to other members of the family, or perhaps by the sea? Don't get too caught up in details at this point, just write down as many ideas and considerations that you think should be made during the moving process. You don't need to work out right now exactly how much garden you need, but you might want to write down that some outside space is important for your new home to include.

Brainstorming should allow you to produce a very long list of things you want in your new home, as well as perhaps things that you need to think a bit more about. This is fine, the next stage will be the part where you weigh your ideas and try to answer any of those lingering questions. For now, just focus on emptying your brain—and the brains of others involved of course—of any relevant information about your new home. Remember, try to resist the temptation to be too specific at this point; just try to get as much down on paper as possible. While you are working through this exercise, don't forget to consider the problem you identified with your current home—how can that be addressed in a new home? What do you need to ensure your new home has so that you do not find yourself in a similar position once you get there?

By the end of this exercise, you should have a fairly long list of all the things that are on your mind (and the minds of other interested parties) about your move. You'll have in front of you a collection of thoughts, desires, wants, and things just to think a bit more about. This is the basis for the next part of the process. You might be surprised by some of the items on your list, as you may not have seen them coming, or even thought of them at all. That is one of the many benefits of brainstorming. It encourages creative and more flexible thinking. In the next chapter, we are going to take this big bag of ideas and start to tighten them up, working out what the actual priorities are, and what items on the list are luxuries that would just be a bonus if it were possible to achieve them.

6

THE NEW HOME BLUEPRINT

In front of you, you should now have a list of characteristics and features you would like your new home to have. There is a good chance that the list is quite lengthy. Don't worry too much about that, as the exercise was just to free up your mind and the minds of others you are moving with, to ensure that you had thought about as many aspects of your new home as possible. You may be looking at some of the items on the list and thinking that they are not realistic, or may not actually be that important in the grander scheme of things.

Well, this is where this chapter comes in. You have produced your long list in the previous chapter, and this chapter is going to help you make sense of all the items on the list. This chapter will run through some processes that will encourage you to think more carefully about each item and weigh just how crucial they are to your happiness and enjoyment in your new home. The idea is that by the end of the chapter you will have a shorter and much more focused list, which contains only the core elements that you actually want in your new home. It will help you see the wood for the trees and make sure that you are not making decisions about new potential homes based on mistaken assessments of importance. Again, this exercise works best when you include others involved in your move. What might not seem very important to you really could make or break the home for another member of your household, and vice versa of course!

The crux of this process is down to one thing. When you consider each item on your list in turn, you need to be able to answer the question "Is this item essential, or is it merely desirable?" Basically, is the presence of this item in your new home so essential that not having it would make the move pointless, unnecessary, or not actually solve the fundamental problem that is triggering your move in the first place? At the end of the process, you will have split your list into two lists. You'll have a list of *essentials* and a list of *desirables,* and each of your items will need to fit under one of those headings.

Of course, it might be that the same item appears on both lists, but in slightly different ways. For example, you may decide that you are not going to move unless you can have a garden (essential). However, you may decide that you are not too concerned about the size of the garden, meaning that a 'large garden' would appear under your list of desirable items. When you are considering your various items, you'll also need to think about time. What I mean by this is that you may eventually want room for two cars on the driveway. However, at the moment, you are content to have one car parked on the driveway and a second in front of the drive (or you may only have one car at the moment). Therefore, under the list of desirable items, you would have 'capacity to make room for two cars on the driveway,' and, under essential, you might have 'room for one car on the driveway.' An example of such a list is below:

Essential	Desirable
Garden	Large garden
Three bedrooms	Four bedrooms
The ability to park one car on the driveway	A study
Capacity in the kitchen for a dishwasher	Room for two cars on the driveway
Upstairs toilet	A summerhouse/shed in the garden
Within five miles of St Leonard's school	Additional toilet downstairs
	Conservatory

This is clearly just a brief hypothetical example (although, when I moved, I was insistent on the dishwasher). Your list may well look very different to this example, which is no surprise given the many different needs people have, as well as the different reasons people move. The benefit of going through this stage of the process is that you will be forced to evaluate every item on your list, and actually arrive at a judgement as to how important to you it actually is. This is really helpful later when you are trying to arrive at conclusions about how good a fit any homes you are viewing are for you. It also assists greatly with reducing the impact of emotion in your decision-making. It leaves you with an objective list of criteria that will help you make the right choice for everyone involved in your move. Without this list, you are leaving yourself vulnerable to deciding about homes based on feelings rather than facts. This can be hugely problematic later, when you might realise you've made a mistake, and you're not in a position to resolve it without significant consequences.

This step of the process might involve just you. However, it may also include any number of other people. If you are planning to share your new home with a partner, then it is likely that they will have a range of opinions about what is going to be essential in a new home and what is going to be less important. It is unlikely that you will agree about absolutely everything when it comes to deciding the importance of various list items, but this does not have to be a problem. It might be that you are content to agree to disagree about some of the items, as some things are not worth the conflict. However, you might be in the difficult position of having very different views about quite important topics that feel less easy to compromise about.

Negotiation (which is likely to be the most helpful tool in these situations) has three main approaches. These approaches, if used properly, can help both parties feel that they have both achieved 'a bit' of what they want, even if not all of it. The key is to try to work towards an agreement that does not leave anyone feeling like they have totally 'lost.'

How can this be achieved? Well, the first option is to reduce the demands (e.g. accepting some outside space of any description if your partner does not view a large garden as essential). The second option is to add conditions (e.g. agreeing with your partner that your new home will only have three bedrooms, and that when child number two comes along, you can purchase an office/shed for the garden so you don't lose your workspace). Negotiation technique number three is completely changing the options (e.g. if both you and your partner favour different houses, write them both off and find a third option you can agree on). These techniques may not solve all the disputes, but they should help with a lot of the smaller pinch points.

Dream Home

This is an exercise that can be helpful in terms of setting out what your absolutely ideal home would include. It is important to note that this is not the same as wishing for a Beverly Hills mansion; it is more about thinking what realistically is the absolute best you could hope for in your next home. To some extent, this might feel like a waste of time, or simply a process of teasing yourself into thinking you can have something that you cannot.

It is not an exercise that all will find helpful, but I know I did. You will need to use your judgement when you have finished reading this section to help decide if it is something you want to try or not. When my wife and I talked about what our personal dream house might look like, what it might include, and all of the various factors involved in that, it was quite enjoyable. We knew the chances of us achieving the 'dream home' were unlikely, but it was something we found useful. When we were at the stage of looking at properties, it was very helpful to have an agreed 'gold standard,' so that we could quite quickly agree where a property was in our list of preferences.

If you have a list of what constitutes a 'dream home' (this will probably be a summary of the 'desirable' elements of your list from the first exercise in this chapter), then you could quickly see if a property was close, or a long way from 'dream home' status. This means you could relatively quickly rule options out completely, or know when a house needed to stay in contention. As stated, it might not be for everyone, but some will find this a useful exercise that can be a great time-saver when the viewings are coming thick and fast.

The main goals of this chapter are to help you to see more clearly what your priorities are. If you follow the steps in this chapter, you should be left with a much clearer, and agreed upon set of priorities for your new home, with those who are making the move with you. Hopefully, you now have a shortlist of essential and desirable or 'bonus' features that your new home will have, and you are in a position to start looking at potential homes. Well done! I expect there has been some negotiation and hard soul searching up to this point. Hopefully, the next parts of the process will be much less stressful because of all of the thinking, planning, and decision-making you have done up to this point.

SECTION III:

MANAGING PEOPLE AND YOUR MOVE

Chapters 7 – 12

7

SEQUENCING

This third part of the book is focused on things you can do to help make the move you are about to embark on as smooth as possible. Some of this is linked to thinking carefully about the process, and what order to do things in, whereas other chapters are focused on how best to manage your working relationships with some of the key players in your move (such as solicitors and estate agents). There are also chapters that deal with the potential minefields that are making and receiving offers for properties, and some of the things to bear in mind during these procedures.

So, what will this chapter be about? Well, as the title of the chapter indicates, we are going to spend some time thinking about what order you should do things in order to make your move as painless and simple as possible. As we know, all people are different, and this means that individuals will have their own preferences about what order to do things in when it comes to moving. As with most of the topics in this book, there is no *right* or *wrong* answer, you need to think about your own personality and the order you need to do things in in order to minimise the stress that moving will cause you. By the end of this chapter, you should have a much better idea of what order you need to do things in.

The greatest risk of getting the sequencing of your move wrong is that you cause yourself unnecessary stress. An example of this comes from my own recent home move. My wife and I were very excited about the prospect of moving to a bigger home, so we went along to a few viewings. This was fine, and it was giving us a good sense of what the market was offering at that time. Then I went and fell in love with a house that I thought was perfect. We even went as far as having an offer accepted. The problem was that we had not sold our flat yet. In fact, we had not even had an offer by this point.

In essence, what I had done was create a huge sense of extra pressure to sell our flat. Of course, another couple came along, liked the house as much as we did and had an offer accepted. The difference was that they were ready to get cracking and were not waiting to sell, so we missed out. I recall being hugely upset about this and believed that I would never find a house I liked as much. Happily, I was wrong, but it goes to show that doing things in the wrong order can cause stress (if you have a similar personality to me). After that experience, my wife and I agreed not to view any more houses until we had accepted an offer on our flat.

Some people would not find themselves so emotionally involved. In that case, it would probably not be a problem to start viewing and looking at potential new homes before you have sold your current home. For me (and many others I expect), however, doing things this way round caused problems. Buying and selling homes is not likely to be an activity you will engage in many times during your life, so you may not know what the right approach is until you have experienced it at least once. Essentially, the sequencing decision is about psychological risk. If you are unlikely to be ruffled by losing homes you have decided you like, view away—the risk of psychological harm to you is low.

Spend some time thinking about what kind of person you are, particularly in terms of patience and tendency to experience feelings of stress. How patient are you in other contexts in your life? If you know you are not a very patient person, it is probably best to wait until you have accepted an offer on your current home before you start looking for your next home in detail. This does not mean you cannot do anything, you can still look online and get a broader sense of how the market is in your desired area, but physically viewing houses may need to be on the back-burner until you have accepted an offer on your current home.

You will also need to consider the personality of others involved in the decision-making about your move. If you are moving with a partner, are they the same as you, or are their needs different? When it comes to psychological wellbeing and avoiding stress, I would always err on the side of caution. If you think you or anyone in your moving party is susceptible to stress, wait until you accept an offer before you start visiting potential future homes.

This chapter might seem like common sense, and, in many ways, it is. However, we often allow ourselves to get swept up in experiences and situations, and we do not always think through the whole process in a way that perhaps we should. You know yourself best and what type of person you are. Use that insight of yourself to think about what approach to take. Others might be able to make suggestions based on what they know about you as well. You might think you are patient, but others may see things differently. Having reached the end of this chapter, you should have the beginnings of a home moving strategy, along with a rough sense of what steps you want to take, and in which order.

8

DEALING WITH ESTATE AGENTS

In this chapter, we are going to consider the role of estate agents. Now, estate agents have not always had the best reputations, but whatever you think about them, they are likely to be a vital ingredient in your move. So, rather than just feel apprehensive or uncertain about your contact with estate agents, this chapter is designed to help you get the best out of your working relationships with these individuals. They remain involved in your move right until you get the keys to the door, so it is well worth nurturing a positive working relationship based on mutual trust and respect, so that you can all achieve your goals.

By the end of this chapter, you should feel well informed about what the role of an estate agent is, how to get the best out of them, how to communicate effectively, and how to ensure that they are being held to account in a productive way that keeps your move on track and your psychological wellbeing protected. They cannot be avoided, so, instead, let's focus on how to maximise the benefits they can offer you during your move.

So, what actually is the job of an estate agent? Effectively, an estate agent is a person or business that arranges the selling, renting, or management of properties and other buildings in the United Kingdom, Ireland, or other countries around the world. An agent that specialises in renting is often referred to as a letting or management agent. Estate agents are mainly engaged in the marketing of property available for sale. In Scotland, however, things are a little different and many solicitors also act as estate agents, a practice that is rare in England and Wales.

Estate agents' fees are generally charged to the seller of the property. Estate agents normally charge the seller, on a 'no sale, no fee' basis, so that if a property doesn't sell, then the customer will not pay anything to the estate agent, and the agent will have worked for the customer up to that point free of charge. If the seller does sell the property and complete the sale of their property to a buyer that was introduced by the estate agent, then the estate agent will charge anything from 1% to 2.5%, with the average being reported as 1.3%. This percentage payment is calculated based on the sale price of the property.

Estate agents seem to have a bit of a bad reputation. They are often considered to be slightly slippery characters that are keen to impress the positive aspects of a property and washing over the problems and more negative features. In films and television programmes, they are likely to be shown describing a pile of rubble as a 'lovely development opportunity' or as 'an older home in need of modernisation.' However, a lot of estate agents are very skilled and serve a number of very important functions during your move. Also, given the high number of estate agencies around the place, they often rely on word of mouth and repeat business, so it really is not in their interests to deliberately mislead you, or cause you extra headaches. So, give them a chance and let the evidence decide how you feel about them; try not to just assume the worst about them.

So, what are the key functions of an estate agent then? They do a number of things that are important to the process of buying and selling a property. They estimate the value of the property, and their knowledge and experience helps them to arrive at 'sensible guesses' about how much you could realistically receive for your own home based on the current market, as well as what you might broadly be able to achieve with your buying budget. They will also market a property if you are selling one. They often work on a 'no sale, no fee' basis, meaning that it is in their interests to get your place sold, and, as they are representing other people who are selling, they have direct lines of communications with people actively looking to move who could well be a good fit for your property.

One of the most important roles they have in the process, and one that is actually very valuable, is their ability to negotiate a deal. They have the ability to agree on a price between yourself and a seller/buyer that suits all (as much as possible). They have the ability to drop in the odd observation that might nudge people in the direction of agreeing to your proposed price, and sellers are much more likely to agree to that with an estate agent than they might with you directly.

I experienced this myself when we were buying our current home. The sellers had rejected our offer of £200,000 (it was on the market for £210,000). They had not made a counter-suggestion, and we were beginning to lose patience. My wife and I had privately agreed that we would not go above £204,000, and I spoke to the estate agent. During that discussion, we agreed that he could offer the seller a range (£202,000 – £203,000). In the end, without any further involvement from us, the estate agent was able to agree on a price of £202,750 with the seller, and, within the hour, we had all agreed and things progressed from there. The estate agent's input at that point was invaluable, and it was a huge stress reliever!

Estate agents don't just wash their hands of you once they have agreed on a price on your behalf. They remain involved in the process until the end. A key function they serve is monitoring the sale/purchase as it proceeds, and they do this by tracking the chain to ensure that any hold ups are smoothed out, and they are also very helpful in terms of keeping you updated about where the chain has become 'stuck' and where the delays are. As part of this function, they will often liaise and stay in touch with mortgage brokers, solicitors, other estate agents, and surveyors.

Estate agents are also likely to be involved in the sale of your property, if indeed you have one to sell. As the experts in this process, they are often well equipped to give you tips about any quick changes you can make to help your home seem more desirable to others, and there is a chance it will then sell more quickly. More generally, experienced estate agents are likely to have a wealth of knowledge about the housing market, both in terms of their own recent sales and those of their competitors. They are a very convenient shortcut to a minefield of information that you would need to access elsewhere if you wanted to avoid dealing with them. They also have access to a lot of other relevant services (surveyors, etc.). So, remember, you are not just working with an estate agent, but also their whole sphere of influence.

The chances are, with an estate agent on board you will sell your home more quickly than trying to do this independently. They are likely to have access to a database of potential buyers, and they will know who could benefit from viewing your place. As moving can be a stressful experience, any way of shaving time off the process can be a blessing! Another reason that you are likely to be able to sell more quickly with an estate agent is that they will be able to take professional photographs of your home, make it look its best, and then be able to place these in suitable places on the Internet, as well as traditional newspaper listings, and their own premises' windows. Placing a property on one of the most widely known Internet property websites can cost up to a thousand pounds a month, so this is advertising that is beyond the reach of most individual and independent home sellers.

As we've established, estate agents have a lot to offer during your move. They have very similar goals to you; they want you to buy or sell, as this is how they get paid! Use this to your advantage and consider them part of your 'moving team.' It is much more psychologically effective to have them on your team, rather than viewing them as an irritant whose main goal is to mislead or deceive you. They operate on word of mouth, a bad service for you could lead to dozens of people not choosing to use their services—people rarely keep their bad customer experiences to themselves. Ultimately, your goals match that of the estate agents. Both you and they want you in a new home and happy. Without this, both of you are at risk of negative consequences, so the natural desire should be to try to avoid such an outcome.

Estate agents are likely to be a vital ingredient in your move. If you work well with them, you could save yourself time and money, and who doesn't want to have as much of those things as possible! You will probably need to suspend judgement a bit. It's easy to get caught up in lazy and stereotypical thinking about them. Force yourself to be fair and work on your own personal experiences. You have a big role in making this relationship work, and if it does, everyone wins!

9

RECEIVING AND ACCEPTING OFFERS

In this chapter, we are going to spend some time exploring what happens when your home is on the market and you start to receive offers. It's always hard to know exactly how popular your home will be or how many viewings you might expect to have after you've decided to sell. It can be a stressful part of the process, especially if you've decided to wait until you have an acceptable offer before you start to view potential new homes for you and your family.

If you've found yourself waiting a while, it can be tempting to impatiently snap the arm off a buyer who comes along with an offer that sounds fairly reasonable. However, as with most home moving decisions, there is often much more to think about rather than just whether you can live with the price tag suggested by the potential buyers.

This chapter will dive down into some of the things to consider when the offers do start to arrive, as well as what you need to be aware of when it comes to receiving offers. This sounds like a passive process, but don't be fooled into thinking that this means that you have no role in it. You are one of the key players, and not having a strategy can leave you vulnerable to losing out on much needed cash, or prematurely accepting an offer that can be problematic later in your move. This chapter will consider some of the key psychological processes that will be essential to securing the right price for you. Use this knowledge well, and you are much more likely to get the positive result you want and deserve.

It is important to remember that not everyone will feel the same way about the home you are leaving as you do. You may have many years' worth of happy memories that have been built up during the time you lived there. Buyers will not. They may see a house that they feel is overpriced or needs a lot of work and, therefore, their offers might reflect this. Remember to keep your feelings in check and do not take low offers personally or as a criticism. A lower offer than the asking price is unlikely to be meant as an insult!

Buyers will have a price in mind that they think is reasonable for the property (just as you will if you are moving on to buy somewhere else), and they do not have the emotional attachment to the home that you will have. No one wants to spend more on something if they don't have to, and this is particularly true if the item is an expensive one, like a house! It is quite normal for buyers to offer 5-10% less than the asking price, so don't be surprised if offers around this level start to come in.

Receiving an offer, especially if you have been waiting for a while, can lead to a sense of urgency. Don't panic, and take your time. Take control of the process by perhaps suggesting that you want to sleep on the offer, which is not an unreasonable request. This will also send the message that you are not going to be harried or harassed into accepting an offer you are not happy with. If you don't take control of the pace of negotiations and discussions, others will try to.

Clearly, information is very useful at this point. Try to talk to the estate agents to get a sense of the buyer's position. Are they in a chain? Do they have a mortgage in principle, or are they perhaps a cash buyer? Are they waiting to sell before they can purchase your property? All of these are important considerations to make when weighing whether to accept an offer or not. It's more than just thinking about whether the price being offered is right; you need to think about the broader implications of accepting the offer for your move.

The first judgement is about price, though. If the offer is much lower than you wanted, one option might be to not make a counter offer. This follows the principles of a psychological process called 'anchoring.' You need to ensure that you are content with where the anchor is placed before haggling and negotiations begin.

For example, imagine you wanted to sell for £150,000, and received an offer of £125,000. You are unlikely to be happy with this offer at all, and you may be tempted to go back and counter suggest £148,000. The difficulty this causes is that the anchor has been set at £125,000, and the likelihood of you getting the buyers to move anywhere close to £150,000 is very small. No one wants to feel like they have moved a huge distance from their starting point. Therefore, ensure you are comfortable with the start point (or 'anchor') before you start making counter offers.

If you receive an offer that is significantly lower than the asking price, and much lower than you are comfortable with, you need to hold your nerve and politely decline the offer, thanking the buyers for their interest. The estate agents can politely explain on your behalf that you were looking for close to the asking price, and then wait to see where their next offer (if there is one) lands. If it is more reasonable (e.g. £140,000), you may decide you are happy to start making counter-suggestions. The 'anchor' is much closer to your valuation now, so the likelihood of you getting a final price you are happy with is improved. If you are not happy, then, again, politely decline and invite them to try again, without offering a price suggestion.

You may feel that you are risking losing the buyers. There is some truth in this, you potentially are. However, the consequence of engaging in discussions when the anchor is too low is that you could end up with a price that is not helpful, or, in extreme circumstances, just plain upsetting! Do not support or engage with a substandard anchor. Ensure that you are driving the process and the pace of negotiations—poker faces and nerves of steel might be necessary, but this is a hugely important transaction, so you need to get it right.

Once you are happy with the price, and before you accept the offer, you need to give some thought to other important issues. What are the relevant timescales? Do your buyers need to move quickly? Do their plans fit with yours? Are they part of a chain? If so, how long is it, and what are the chances of successful completion in this case? Do the buyers have any flexibility in how they can manage the transaction? As you can see, price is one aspect of a set of broader decisions and judgements that need to be made when deciding whether to accept an offer on your home. If you yourselves are in a hurry, you may not want to accept an offer from buyers who are in a long chain and who do not yet have a mortgage arranged, especially if there are rival bids from cash buyers who are not in a chain.

When the time comes and you conclude that you can feel confident that the right thing to do is accept an offer, then you can do this through your estate agents. The next stage involves surveys or home inspections, and these can sometimes lead to surprise findings. If this happens on a property you are selling, don't be surprised if the buyers return to you with a view to re-negotiating the price. It's worth not being too stubborn at this point—if a leaky roof has come up in one survey, it is likely to come up in a different one too. So, either bite the bullet and re-negotiate, or withdraw from negotiations, pay for the repair yourself, and then return to the market. Remember, nothing is legally binding until contracts have been exchanged.

In summary, receiving and sifting through offers can be a tricky part of the process, with a number of ever-changing considerations to make. Your role is being clear in your own mind about what price you can live with in order to sell your home. Use this as your marker and make sure that it is you who are controlling (as much as possible) where the anchor gets laid. This can feel stressful, especially if offers are few and far between, but remember that this stress is likely to be much more short-lived than any stress attached to selling to the wrong buyer, or selling for the wrong price. These stresses can be much longer lasting and more damaging.

10

VIEWING HOMES

This chapter is going to focus on the next stage of the home moving process: viewing potential future homes. This can be a difficult step for a number of reasons. It might be that your key requirements are not clear (this won't be the case if you followed the process described in chapters five and six of this book). It might be the case that emotions are getting in the way of your thinking, and that this is leading to disagreements between yourself and any others involved in the process. Finally, it might be the case that you are struggling to make a choice between two or more very similar properties and cannot settle on which one to proceed with.

This chapter will seek to address all of the problems described above. In this chapter, we will explore a number of things you can do to help mitigate the impact of emotions and difficulties around decision-making. There are a number of different ways of making decisions about your future home, but I will introduce one that I found incredibly helpful when my wife and I were choosing our current home. The process I am going to discuss will help you drill down into the detail and help remove some of the emotion from the decision.

You don't need me to tell you how important a decision about moving is likely to be, and what the consequences might be of making a choice that ultimately works out to be wrong for you and your loved ones. It is the very definition of a decision that you only want to make correctly, and most importantly, only once. Getting it wrong could lead to negative financial and emotional consequences, so an objective and level-headed approach at this point in the process is crucial. By the end of the chapter, you will have learned about one method of making this decision that surgically removes the emotion and ensures that your choice is as objective as it is ever going to be. You might choose to use only one aspect of the approach, or you might use both—either way, you can feel confident that you are moving closer to a decision that is going to be right for you.

As I mentioned earlier, emotion can be a real problem when it comes to significant life choices such as choosing your home. Emotions are awesome and clearly a wonderful part of the human experience, but they can also be a fly in the ointment of clear and logical decision-making. Getting carried away with feelings of excitement might mean that we overlook less positive aspects of a home, similarly they could lead us to end up with a property that requires a huge investment to repair or renovate. This is why keen emotional management and striving for meaningful and genuine objectivity is so central to effective decision-making when we are home hunting. Below are some ways of ensuring that you are being as objective as possible.

The Policeman

I don't literally mean a policeman. I'm not suggesting you go out, grab a copper and then frogmarch him around the houses you are viewing. I'm talking more about an objective, emotion policeman (or woman) here. Basically, it can be useful to have someone involved in the process who is more emotionally detached, for all the reasons we have already covered. Memories can be unreliable, and later, when you are trying to weigh the various pros and cons of the possible homes you have viewed, you may misremember, or inaccurately remember certain aspects (e.g. size of bedrooms etc.). This might be because you are so wrapped up and in love with a property that you cannot see it as anything other than perfect, or just because your memory is not great.

Whatever the reason for your wonky view, the policeman can help. This person can help to remind you about what you actually saw, as well as hopefully serve to supply some home truths if necessary. Therefore, this is quite an important role, and should only really be assigned to someone you trust and who is able to be honest with you, regardless of how much you want them to support your potentially warped view of a property. Do not choose a mouse for this role, the person needs to be able to speak their mind, and put you straight if this is necessary. This helps to bypass some of the emotion that might be impacting your view—an objective person who won't be living there will help to ensure you are being sensible and pragmatic in your judgements.

The Property Scorecard

This is the tool that will really help you make sense of how you are objectively evaluating the various features of the homes you are considering. You will have already identified your personal priorities if you have followed the suggestions in chapters five and six. You will need this information now as you begin to assess the homes you are viewing. Please see Figure 2 for an example of a completed property scorecard.

	The differing impact of sub-totals for each category allows the significance of each category to be accounted for during the decision process.	Grass Avenue	Summer Road	Quarry Road	North Road	West Street
MUST HAVES	Room for two cars to park	9	8	7	9	2
	Space for a dishwasher	7	9	6	5	9
	Three bedrooms	5	9	8	4	9
	Outside space	5	5	5	5	5
	Score total for Must Haves	26	31	26	23	25
	Weighted (x6) total for Must Haves	**156**	**186**	**156**	**138**	**150**
W A N T S	Reasonably sized garden	4	9	4	7	9
	Big kitchen	5	8	0	7	4
	Dining room	6	5	8	8	8
	Entrance hall / porch	6	7	8	8	6
	Close to Oakfield school	4	7	4	8	2
	Close to a shop	5	5	5	5	5
	Score total for Wants	30	41	29	43	34
	Weighted (x3) total for Wants	**90**	**123**	**87**	**129**	**102**
NICE TO HAVE	Attractive area	7	9	8	6	5
	New boiler	8	7	8	8	5
	Limited refurbishment required	5	2	6	8	5
	Garden shed	5	8	5	5	9
	Score total for Nice to Have	25	26	27	27	24
	Weighted (x1) total for Nice to Have	**25**	**26**	**27**	**27**	**24**
	Grand (weighted) totals	**271**	**335**	**270**	**294**	**276**

Figure 2: Property Scorecard

The first thing to say is that this scorecard is not as complicated as it may appear. Below, I will explain the process to follow in order to complete your own property scorecard (a printable pdf version of the property scorecard is available for download for free at the end of this book).

1. Add in all of your requirements (taken from your new home blueprint, Chapter 6) and add them under one of the above categories as *must haves, wants,* or *nice to have.* As you can imag-

ine, the more important a feature is, the higher the category it should be placed in.

2. As you view properties, insert a score for each item into the column relating to that property. Scores should be awarded out of 10 for how well that property fulfils that particular criterion. For example, a house that has a dishwasher installed and is being left in the house by the sellers when they leave would probably get a 9 or 10. A house that had a readymade space for a dishwasher might get a 7. A property where one could be fitted but this has not yet occurred might get a 5, and a property that has no dishwasher and no way of installing one would probably get a 0.

3. Now for the maths! Use the weighted score guides to calculate the totals for each of the three categories.

4. Add the three scores together to give you a total score for that property.

5. Follow the same process for all of the properties you view.

What you should end up with is a comprehensive analysis of a number of different properties, which have resulted in each being given a clear score. This is a simple, but powerful approach, and as you can see, makes it easy to rank the different properties based on the facts, rather than emotions. If you wanted to be even more scientific, you could involve your 'policeman' in the scoring of the various criteria (providing they have viewed the properties with you). Once you have completed this process, you will be able to see the wood for the trees, and start to think about which properties, if any, you want to make an offer for.

So, in summary, you are likely to find it beneficial to have a person or a process (preferably both) that will help you to ensure that your decision-making is objective, and that you are not being unduly impacted upon by your emotions. Feelings can get in the way, and I'm sure we can all remember occasions when we allowed ourselves to get carried away by the excitement of an idea, and moving can definitely lead to these feelings. This is why tools like those covered in this chapter can be so important. The tools described here are suggestions, and by no means an exhaustive list. Whatever you do, take a moment to check your thinking. Can you be completely confident you are acting with a cool head and a dispassionate viewpoint?

11

MAKING AN OFFER

Okay, so you've been through a careful selection process, and have objectively decided on a property that you have concluded meets the needs of you and your moving party. You have arrived at this conclusion after careful and mindful analysis; well done you! Now is the time then, for making an offer. This might seem like quite a straightforward part of the process, and, in some ways, it is. However, there are potential complications here that need to be evaluated and explored before you start chucking hypothetical money around.

As has already been mentioned, buying a home is a huge commitment that has significant consequences for your life in a number of different but equally important ways. Therefore, it is a decision you need to get right the first time, and you need to ensure that you are not overpaying for a home—something that can cause problems for years to come. This chapter, hereafter, is written with these issues in mind. Consider it a non-exhaustive list of things to consider and weigh, as well as a guide to managing the art of negotiation from the buying (rather than selling) side.

So, what should you be considering when making an offer?

The condition of the property is an important factor. It might be that the survey has thrown up new issues that you were previously unaware of, and this knowledge can often leave you in a good negotiating position when it comes to discussing an offer. It might be that the sellers will accept a lower offer in recognition of the need to spend money on repairs, or that they keep the price the same but agree to get the work done before you buy (and you will require proof of completion before the sale is finalised).

What have similar properties in the area sold for? There are websites that allow you to check selling history in the area, and these websites can be excellent ways of letting the sellers know that their asking price may not be realistic for the area, and that there is a ceiling that they are unlikely to break in terms of price. Your estate agent will also have an idea about how flexible the sellers are likely to be on price, as well as how long the property has been on the market. A property that has not sold for a while, and has had limited viewings, could be available at a reduced price. Googling the address might also give away the fact that the property has been listed with a number of estate agents—a clue that it has been difficult to sell.

Of course, if you have seen a property that you consider your dream home, and you can afford the asking price without putting an unnecessary strain on your finances, you would be wise not to mess around. There is often multiple interest in properties, and, if one is perfect for you, there is a good chance it will be perfect for others too. Don't get too caught up in snapping up a bargain to the extent that you miss out on the perfect home. Pride comes before the fall remember; don't let this get in the way of landing the perfect home for you. There is no shame in offering the asking price on the right home for you, this does not equate to you 'losing.'

Of course, it might be that your initial offer is rejected. Don't be too disheartened if this happens, as it is quite normal for below asking price offers to be rejected, as the sellers will want to get as close to their asking price as possible. However, this is where anchoring can again work in your favour. If you can get a counter offer then you have set the anchor, and this will be in everyone's mind throughout the negotiation. The estate agents can be pivotal here. They may represent the sellers at this point, but they are likely to have a good knowledge of the types of offers that are going to be favourably received. It's also important not to allow yourself to be rushed. You may feel pressure to go back with an increased offer, but it might be wise to sleep on it for a day or two.

Once you have had an offer accepted, then the seller may choose to take the property off the market. This is something that you can request happens once you have an offer accepted, but the seller may reserve the right to keep the property on the market to see if they get an even better offer than the one they accepted from you. If the seller wants to take this approach, that might indicate that they are not fully committed to selling to you; so, give this situation careful consideration if this is where you find yourself. In the United Kingdom, there is no legal obligation to follow through on the agreement until late in the process, when contracts are exchanged.

In summary, making an offer can be a complicated and nerve-wracking process. Your main role at this point is to ensure that any offers you are making are logical and financially viable in both the short- and long-term. You also need to hold your nerve, make sure that, as much as possible, you are controlling the speed of negotiations and keep your cards close to your chest. Also, do not try to save yourself an inconsequential amount of money for reasons of pride, missing out on a home that would be hard to match in terms of fitting with the needs of your family for the sake of a smallish amount of money; this is likely to be hard to recover from.

12

DEALING WITH SOLICITORS

In this chapter, we are going to spend time considering another important member of your moving team, your solicitor. Just as it is very difficult to move without getting involved in some way with estate agents, if you are selling or purchasing a property, it is even less likely that you are going to be able to achieve the goal of moving without the involvement of a solicitor.

Much like estate agents, solicitors can get a hard time and an unfriendly description from people who have dealt with them in the process of moving. They can be described as indifferent, apathetic, and only focused on the money. Some of these things may be true at times, but they could also be considered to be quite logical; why should a stranger you do not know be worried about you moving and prioritise that over other work? Whatever the approach of your solicitors, this chapter will consider ways that you can to maximise the efficiency of that relationship, as well as maintaining the integrity and functionality of the working relationship.

Solicitors are an important part of your move if you are purchasing a property. The process of buying property requires conveyancing, which is the name of all of the legal processes that surround buying a property—this work can only be conducted appropriately and legally by a solicitor. Their work (in the United Kingdom at least) involves dealing with the Land Registry, stamp duty charges and payments, drawing up and assessing contracts, any necessary legal advice, and transfer of the funds involved in your purchase. Things operate a little differently in Scotland, so it is worth searching for more local guidance and information there.

Choosing a solicitor is an unglamorous, yet important stage in the home buying process. No matter what your estate agent tells you, you really are under no obligation to work with the in-house solicitors they may have, or the ones they recommend. A cautionary tale here—when selling our flat, the buyer went with the solicitor recommended by the estate agent. She was slow and inefficient, and it later came to light that she had offered all of the local estate agents a set fee for referrals to her. Make your own decision in terms of solicitors.

It might be worth finding and using a 'fixed-fee' service, which means you only pay the amount that is quoted when you sign up. This avoids unpleasant surprises further down the line. If possible, try to avoid engaging a solicitor who is very busy; you would much prefer someone who can give your case proper attention. If it is possible, tell the solicitor your preferred exchange and completion dates and ask if they can meet these deadlines. A final point is to try not to make your choice for a solicitor based purely on price. This is clearly going to be a consideration, but the solicitor you select will be responsible for all of the legal work surrounding your property purchase, and if they miss anything or make a mistake, it could end up costing you a lot more than the amount you saved by choosing the cheapest service.

Solicitors cost money. You can expect to pay anywhere between £500 and £1,500 for the conveyancing alone, which won't include stamp duty and other costs associated with the property purchase. The cost will also depend on how complex the property transaction is. For example, if the property is a leasehold, there's more legal work to do. This means the price is likely to be higher. Some solicitors will charge a flat fee, whereas others will charge a fee based on a percentage of the value of the property. It is always worth getting a few quotes to help inform your choice.

One of the biggest problems with solicitors can be that they can be 'relaxed' in how they approach the work. To combat this in part, it is always worth asking friends and family about their experiences—word of mouth is often a great tool to uncover hidden gems! Often, solicitors can command a degree of respect because of their trade, and this can mean that people forget that solicitors are humans just like us! More importantly, they are humans who are working for us, and as we are paying their wages, we are entitled to know what is happening, and it is not unreasonable to expect an efficient and well-communicated service (especially given the amount the service costs).

You need to get the balance right. There is no point badgering your solicitor so much that they don't actually have time to do the work you are paying them for! However, regular updates are not unreasonable, and it might be worth sending a weekly email (on the same day of the week) to ask for an update. This helps to let the solicitor know that you expect to be kept updated, and it will also help to develop a culture of the solicitor needing to have something to update you with— subliminal messages like this can be very powerful and effective. However, remain polite and respectful. This will also help to motivate progress. There is a chance your polite requests might lead to snappy or irritable responses. Don't be fazed by this—you are not being unreasonable and can rightly expect an update.

In summary, solicitors are crucial if you are buying property. It might feel like there is no urgency for them, and, in fairness, there isn't! However, you are paying for their service. This means you need to do your homework and make a good choice in the first place. Then, a process of steady and consistent, but polite, requests for updates are the best recipe for a successful working relationship with this member of your moving team.

SECTION IV:
ACTUALLY MOVING

Chapters 13 – 15

13

PLANNING FOR MOVING DAY

So, you've decided a move will improve your life and solve a problem. You've chosen your new home, and you're now ready to start the process of physically moving. Easy right? Sadly, probably not! There is a reason that moving is widely accepted as being one of the most stressful things you can do in life. Your life, luckily only temporarily, is almost literally going to be turned upside down until you are settled in your new home. Therefore, you need to ensure that you have some things in place to help make this process as serene as possible.

This chapter will include a combination of practical tips and thinking approaches that mean you will be well set to moving in a way that will reduce the amount of stress you can expect to experience. By the end of this chapter, you will have an idea of what to expect and what to consider, so that your actual moving day can be calm and focused, and so that you do not end up in a conflict that means you could be living in your new home alone!

So, what things can you do to help reduce the stresses of moving day? Organisation is normally a good way of ensuring that you are unlikely to experience undue levels of stress, and this might involve things like calling around to your moving team and asking for their help well in advance of moving day. The sooner they know when they are needed, the more likely they are to be able to help.

Think about what each person who is moving needs on the day. Young children might be best being entertained for the day, perhaps being taken for a day out by an aunt, an uncle, or a family friend while the physical moving is happening. What is going to happen to the cat? Perhaps they could go into a pet care facility for 48 hours until the worst is over and they can safely re-join the family.

Your moving team (I'm talking specifically here about willing volunteers) are giving up their precious free time to engage in manual labour and hang around in what can be a stressful context. Look after them. Ensure they remain well fed and watered throughout the day. This helps to keep spirits up and demonstrates your gratitude; it also ensures they will be more likely to help out with teething problems that are likely to crop up before too long!

If possible, some preparation at your new home can be helpful and avoid unnecessary stress. Ensure you have enough light bulbs for your new place, and think about putting cardboard down to protect flooring and walls where necessary. You'll appreciate this later when there is too much thudding and banging going on during the move. Buy some freezer bags and put screws and fittings into these, attaching them to the relevant piece of furniture securely—again, this will avoid problems finding lost screws when reassembling in your new home.

You might want to think about a moving day *survival pack*. This should include things like a box cutter, paper towels, bin bags, cutlery, toilet paper, the kettle, and some mugs as well as tea, coffee, milk, and sugar. A cup of tea/coffee is likely to be high on the agenda on moving day when you and your team have been hard at it for hours on end! One particularly helpful thing to do is to take photographs of the back of televisions and other electrical items—this will be invaluable when it comes to reconnecting everything at your new home. This tip can also apply to any decorative or ornamental arrangements you want to recreate in your new home.

In summary, moving day can be a stressful experience. It makes sense to think methodically about what each member of your moving party is going to need and want on the day. If you can prepare as much as possible to meet these needs, then the basics are covered and most catastrophes can be avoided. Plan for the day as much as you can and consider some of the tricks above to help cut out unnecessary stress—this is the key to a peaceful and serene moving experience. Look after your moving team, as every one of them is giving up some of their precious time, so make sure they know you appreciate it, and they'll be there to help you with your next move!

14

DECLUTTERING

This chapter is going to focus on the process of decluttering. This sounds like an inherently practical task, and in many ways it is, so there are a few practical tips about how to do this. However, the great nemesis of decluttering is hoarding, and this is something that can be a real barrier to decluttering, which is often an important part of any home move.

This is why we are going to spend some time looking at what can cause hoarding, and what can be done about it. Moving is a tricky business, and if we can make it easier by reducing the amount of physical stuff we actually have to transport, then this can only be a good thing.

So, what is hoarding then? Well, it is generally understood to be a difficulty in being separated from items (and sometimes animals) and developing an intense emotional attachment to them, which acts as a blocker to trying to remove the items from our lives. Sometimes hoarding can become very problematic, to the extent that the hoarders themselves no longer have any idea what they have in their possession, or where they might find certain items that they have been accumulating.

Hoarders may worry about discarding an item and then

needing it at a later point. The difficulty in accurately assessing the chances of needing something in the future means that the risk averse choice is made, and the item is, more often than not, retained. Sometimes, hoarders have experienced a degree of trauma in their lives, and this means that they begin to transfer that trauma to items, and feel that disposing of items somehow reinforces or triggers the trauma, leaving them emotionally vulnerable, and therefore less inclined to part with their possessions, regardless of their actual use or value.

Experts who have conducted research with individuals who struggle with hoarding behaviours have learned through the use of brain scans that these people begin to experience elevated levels of anxiety when being asked to make decisions about throwing things away. The research also interestingly concluded that hoarders made very pragmatic decisions when asked to choose items to throw away belonging to others, but could not apply this pragmatic approach to their own possessions.

It is clear that some people can really struggle with the process of decluttering. It is useful to know that if this is the case with yourself, or someone you know, and you may be helping with the move, there is often a deeper reason, and the chances that they are being belligerent for the sake of it are quite small. Be patient, and apply some of the tips below and, hopefully, progress will be made.

A basic approach to decluttering would involve taking a room at a time and having categories to place items in, such as *keep*, *sell*, and *bin/recycle/donate*. Take each item in turn and ask yourself if you have used it in the last 6, or even 12 months. If you haven't, can you see yourself using it in the next 12 months? If you don't think you will, does it really need to move with you? Can you make some money from it, or is it just worthless and taking up space? This process will help you start to make informed choices about what to keep and what to throw away or sell.

It is not always possible, but, ideally, a process of decluttering should occur several weeks before the actual moving day. This means that you are less likely to be rushed, and more likely to be able to feel that you are making reasonable decisions about what items you are keeping or discarding. Try to make sure you have time to focus on this task. Done properly, it will save you time and money in the long run.

As you are organising the items in your home, as well as asking yourself how much you need something, and how likely it is that you will need it, also ask yourself what would happen if you needed it but did not have it? If not having it meant that you needed to pop to the shop and spend a few pence to replace the item, perhaps it is not absolutely essential that it travel with you to your new home.

Decluttering is a useful process that helps to streamline and organise your life, and when you are moving to a new home is an ideal time to get involved in such a task. Parting with things can be a wrench, but it can also be quite liberating. Try to think rationally and logically about your possessions. Do you actually need all of them, or could they be better used and appreciated elsewhere? Not only might you achieve a nice sense of wellbeing helping others, but you might also make a little cash, and you will certainly be making your move a lot less stressful.

15

MOVING DAY

This chapter is going to cover the day of the actual move. This can be an emotionally draining day, as it is both exciting to move onto new pastures and very tiring, as you try to ensure that everything goes smoothly, as you transport your worldly possessions to your new home. The process would have been made somewhat simpler by the diligent and focused decluttering that, hopefully, has occurred, but this process alone is unlikely to eradicate all stresses from the day.

As the actual move is the culmination of a broader stressful process, it would be a shame to have this part feel like an unpleasant experience. Therefore, this chapter is going to include some top tips on staying organised to reduce stresses, as well as ways in which you can avoid any unnecessary stress during this stage of the process. This is important, as mistakes at this point can cause real headaches later, so if they can be avoided in the first place, this is clearly ideal.

As with much of the process that has been covered so far, organisation is very important in keeping moving day as serene and stress free as possible. Make sure you get an early night before moving day—good sleep will help to avoid tiredness and unhelpful tetchiness. Snapping at those who have volunteered to help is unlikely to be responded well to. Another thing it might be useful to do the night before is make sure you have a rough timetable of what is happening and when. This will help you outline where people need to be at what time, and what it is they will be doing. This provides you with a bit of a schedule that you can use when you call around to confirm with your moving team what they are doing.

As previously stated, hopefully, you have identified a member of your moving team that can entertain and look after any young children or pets. You will need to ensure that if anyone needs to get into your new home before you, that you have given them keys to access it, or that there is a person to let them in. A situation where movers sit outside your new home unable to start unloading is a real timewaster, and this will inevitably lead to frustration. If you have provided your movers with a desired floor plan of your new home, the rooms can start to take shape before you even arrive!

It might be worth locating all of your most important documents (such as driving licences, passports, birth certificates etc.) and putting them in an envelope, perhaps to be stored with a trusted member of your moving party until you are fully installed in your new home. If you are able to get to your new home, it is a good idea to have a quick scout around to make sure all of the fixtures and fittings are as you expect them to be, and that any furniture negotiated has been left as agreed. Take photographs of anything that you believe is not as it should be for solicitors at a later point.

When you are in your new home, you need to start unpacking the most important and regularly used items first. This might include crucial kitchen appliances, some clothes, bed linen, bathroom essentials, and towels. It's not always possible, but if you have a storage area somewhere else, a gradual moving in and organising of boxes is a great way of managing the stresses of a move and avoiding a cluttered environment. It's not ideal if you're missing a crucial item though!

On the day of the move, it probably makes sense to ensure you have a phone on you so you are contactable for emergencies and to keep in touch with other factions of your moving party. Stay hydrated, and don't forget to eat. You don't want to become unwell because of dehydration or a lack of fuel in the middle of your moving day. It's likely that a lot of your friends and family will know you are moving, and they are going to be part of your moving team. However, if they are not helping with the move, it would be a good idea to let them know that you are going to be busy on that day and should probably not be disturbed unless it is an emergency. Distractions during this day can be unwelcome and add to the stress.

In summary, moving day itself should be an exciting and focused day. It can be stressful though, so a few well-placed pieces of communication and planning beforehand can contribute enormously in terms of making the day more relaxed and less hectic. The more you can put in place in advance the better, and remember to be kind to yourself and your moving team. Plenty of drinks, snacks, and jokes will go a long way to keeping everyone cheery and keen to help.

SECTION V:

PSYCHOLOGICAL WELLBEING AND MOVING

Chapters 16 – 18

16

MOVE LIKE A SURGEON

It has already been stated a number of times throughout this book that moving can be a very stressful process. Therefore, this chapter is focused on the idea of moving like a surgeon. This might sound a bit vague, but the basic concept is that in order to avoid stress, it is best to image yourself to be someone who will not necessarily entertain emotions during the process, and that's easier said than done. It might not be possible to eradicate emotional responses during the process of moving, but it should be possible to reduce their presence and impact.

Why is this an important thing to invest time in considering? Well, the links between out of control emotions and impulsive decision-making and behaviour are fairly well established. In short, the more we allow emotions to cloud our judgement, the more likely we are to make choices that may not be in our best interests in the long run. That is why it is important we do our best to reduce the role of emotions in our moving process.

If you were about to undergo surgery under general anaesthetic, you would probably want this to be conducted by a surgeon, not just because they have all the relevant training and experience (although this clearly helps), but because, in general, surgeons are masters of completing very complex and demanding tasks without a sniff of emotion. I cannot imagine that an overly emotional or panicky surgeon would fare well cutting through flesh and bones to perform intricate surgery requiring the steadiest hand and most serene and focused mind-set. Imagine counting down towards unconsciousness and noticing that your surgeon seemed stressed and on edge —that's not something that would leave you confident and calm!

Surgeons can perform well under intense pressure for a number of reasons. One of the most important reasons is likely to be their ability to compartmentalise—to keep their emotions in check and stop them interfering with the task at hand. This is what you should aspire to when it comes to your move. How can this be achieved? We're not robots. Well, there are a number of things to think about, which should help you to work towards a state of Zen-like serenity.

Wherever possible, stick to facts and numbers. What I mean by this is throughout the process, if you have followed the steps suggested in this book, you should feel fairly confident and comfortable with the decisions you have made to this point. For example, you should have settled on a new home that achieved the highest score out of the ones you looked at. This means that you know, factually and objectively, you made the best decision you could at that point. Remembering things like this can help greatly with anxiety. Remind yourself of how you arrived at each choice on the journey, and then any sneaky doubts or worries will be much easier to challenge.

Strive for collaboration throughout your move. There will be flashpoints. There are going to be times when you, and other members of your moving party, and your moving team will not see eye to eye. Accept that others will have different views and strive for common ground and compromise. Often, just feeling listened to can be a powerful way of diffusing stressful and emotional points.

Finally, planning is something that can really reduce the amount of stress that you encounter during the moving process. You cannot predict everything that is going to happen, life does not work like that, but the more planning you can do at the right points in the process means that you are likely to avoid undue stresses, and you can maintain that surgeon-like approach to your move.

In summary, to avoid stress during your move, imagine you are a hardened surgeon and the patient on the operating table is your home move. You want to approach this process calmly, in a way that focuses on numbers and facts, and leaves emotions at the door of the operating theatre. Emotions can interfere with clear thinking, so the best approach is to try to reduce the impact of these, and waiting until you can enjoy huge feelings of relief and excitement when you are popping champagne corks in your new home. I'm not saying that none of the process will be enjoyable. I think I'm highlighting the need to monitor your stress levels and ensure you are doing everything you can to use objective data, as opposed to raw emotions, to make important choices and decisions.

17

THE WAITING GAME

Who likes waiting? Not many people, and when it's a life-changing event like a home move that you are waiting for, it can feel even more stressful and emotionally draining to have to wait. Moving is a complex process that is filled with the need to wait. Therefore, it is important to be aware of what the timescale might be for the process, so that you are prepared and able to cope with the parts of the process that involve mostly waiting on others.

Knowing how long a move is going to take is a tricky concept. Each moving process is so unique, that rules of thumb are not always that easy to feel confident in. Nevertheless, as of 2018, the following are the kinds of timescales that you can expect to be subject to. On average, a process of selling and buying a home tends to last anywhere between six weeks and three months. Having a purchase property in a chain can of course make things take longer. Here are the stages of a move with expert guidance as to how long these stages tend to take:

- Selling your current home – 4 to 10 weeks
- Organising a mortgage – 2 weeks

- Choosing a new home – 1 to 12 weeks
- Conveyancing and surveys – 4 to 12 weeks
- Moving and settling in – 1 to 2 weeks

The above are ballpark figures and individual circumstances mean that these could all be different for you depending in your situation. These stages do not always happen in a uniform order of course. Some of the stages overlap and some cannot occur without other things happening first, so that can affect the timeline of your move significantly.

The key with moving and having to wait and rely so much on others for parts of the process is achieving a degree of serenity. This is easier said than done, and you will need to police yourself and other members of your moving party in this sense. What can you do to help them manage their stresses and stay patient, and what can you do for yourself?

One useful thing to consider might be ensuring that you are on top of your to-do list. Hopefully, this book will have given you plenty of hints about the need to plan and get organised. Are there future stages that you could be preparing for? Could you be decluttering gradually as you wait for a completion date? Could you be drumming up support and calling in favours ready for the big move? Could you be finalising and agreeing the scorecard for your new home to act as a guide when you are viewing, as you are waiting to accept a suitable offer for the home you are selling?

You could use slower parts of the process to research solicitors and get quotes from them. You could do some light research of friends and family to see who they recommend. Normally, there is always something to do whilst moving, so a much healthier way of managing the wait is to be constructive and productive, and use the time wisely to help progress and control the parts of the process you can. This is crucial, as so much of the process is not in your hands; this is where the stress and negative emotions can really be powerful and most problematic.

It can often be useful to think about all the stages of the process you have already completed. That can help to reassure you that you have moved forward, and if you have taken the steps following the suggestions in this book, you can also feel confident that you are likely to have made sensible and logical decisions that are right for you and the rest of your moving party. Give yourself a pat on the pack. You are making great choices!

Moving can be a long process, with several periods where you are simply waiting for other people to do their parts of the process. These can be really frustrating times, but there are things you can do to help minimise the frustration and anxiety you may end up experiencing. Remind yourself of how far you have come to date, and try to stay on top of your to-do list. That's probably the best you can do to avoid stress caused by waiting.

18

STRESS MANAGEMENT

What can you do if the stress is getting on top of you? Sometimes we can try our best to keep it at bay and make sure we are not carelessly inviting stress in, but we are only human, and sometimes our best efforts fall short. If this happens, we might benefit from stress management techniques to help us reduce the impact and consequences of this stress, so that we can ensure we are working back towards a more level-headed and balanced approach that has been the theme of this book.

This chapter has lots of suggestions for practical things that you can do to help reduce your stress levels once they start to rise. This book has covered the reasons why avoiding and managing stress is important in the process of moving, and this is why this chapter can be a useful source of ideas should stress become an issue.

Effective stress management often involves quite simple and practical techniques, and below is a list of some of these ideas:

- Breathing

Breathing more deeply and slowly will help to slow your heart rate and allow you to feel more in control of the situation (or at least yourself). Stress is often linked to a feeling of not being in control, so reclaiming a sense of empowerment is an important goal to strive for. When you feel your stress levels rising, find a quiet space on your own and take some long and deep breaths.

- Walking (staying active)

Exercise is a great way of clearing your mind. I'm at my calmest and most rational after a good run. The fresh air and endorphins work wonders for stress, and these endorphins counteract stress hormones. Walking through nice open green spaces also helps to free up your mind to relax and focus on more positive ways of thinking about your situation and moving forward.

- Listen to soothing music

One of the simplest stress management techniques is to listen to some soothing music. This can mean different things to different people, of course, but listen to whatever music helps you to feel relaxed. Listening to music will lower your heart rate and reduce your blood pressure. Music floods the brain with feel-good neurochemicals, like dopamine, and that will reduce anxiety and stress fast.

- Stay hydrated

This might seem like an odd one, but not having enough water in our systems can do all kinds of funny things to us. Therefore, it is helpful to stay on top of your water intake and ensure that you are topped up. This will help your body cope with stress hormones and reduce the chances that they will be as problematic as they might otherwise be. Dehydration, even by levels as low as seventeen fluid ounces (just over two glasses) increases cortisol levels in your body, and cortisol is the hormone your body produces in response to stress.

- Keep talking

There is a good chance that there are other people in your moving party. They are also likely to be experiencing levels of stress, although possibly to differing degrees than you, depending on how involved they are with the decision-making and organisation of the move. Share your experiences with each other. It is often quite validating and reassuring to know that you are not alone in feelings stressed or worked up. Knowing you are not alone is a sure-fire way of reducing stress.

- Eat well

In addition to ensuring you remain hydrated, ensure that you are eating properly and keeping your body fuelled with goodness and avoid the junk! Diets that are high in fibre and lower in saturated fats have been shown to have a positive impact on mood. Vitamin B is also great for managing a low mood, so healthier foods, such as lean chicken, spinach, and fish, are amongst some of the best things to eat.

- Mediation / mindfulness

These techniques will not work for everyone, but if you are someone who finds them beneficial, ensure you are making time for these activities. Moving can involve lots of rushing around, and a lot of decision-making and brain power. It is even more useful then, to sit back and give yourself time to recharge your brain.

In summary, we know moving can be stressful. This book is designed to give you the best possible chance of avoiding unnecessary stress and retaining a sense of calm and control throughout the process. However, we are all only human, and that means that sometimes, despite our best efforts, we are not successful in avoiding stress as much as we would like.

In this instance, the tips in this chapter should be useful in terms of reducing any stress you are experiencing. They may not rid you of it completely, but they will help to minimise and keep it in check, which can in itself avoid further problems. Not all the tips will work for everyone—you may need to try a few to see what works for you through a process of trial and error.

19

NEXT STEPS

At the start of this book, I made you a promise.

I promised that if you followed the advice and suggestions in this book, you would be in a position to move to a new home calmly and serenely, and that you would feel confident about all of the decisions you had made along the way. I promised that you would be much more likely to get through your move with less conflict, and that you would feel much more in control of the whole process.

One of the key parts of the promise was that you needed to follow the guidelines and suggestions made in this book.

I'm not going to lie and tell you that this book is a magic wand, or that moving is going to be absolutely stress free. However, following the steps in this book will have been a great start in helping you to move calmly and successfully.

I stand by my promise. I am confident that the material in this book can make a big difference to your move, and for the other people involved in your move.

Enjoy your new home. You've earned it.

FREE PRINTABLE POSTER TO HELP YOU MAKE SURE YOU CHOOSE THE RIGHT HOME!

This book has covered a range of techniques and ideas to help make your house move successful and stress free.
One of the most important tools described in the book is the property scorecard, which you can download and print if you follow the link below:

https://mailchi.mp/531a5f7efee7/go22zqr6so

Please download the pdf, print it out as many times as you need it (one per prospective home) and feel confident that you have made the right choice!

Thank you for reading my book. If you enjoyed it, you can make a big difference.

Reviews are the most powerful tools in my arsenal when it comes to getting attention for my books. Much as I'd like to, I don't have the financial muscle of a New York or London publisher. I can't take out full page ads in the newspaper or put posters on the subway.

But I'd like to think I have something more powerful and effective than that, and it is something that most writers would love to get their hands on.

A kind and helpful bunch of readers.

I really appreciate all of your feedback, and I love hearing what you have to say. I need your input to make the next version better, and to help my career as a writer. Honest reviews of my books help bring them to the attention of other readers they could help.

If you've enjoyed this book or found it helpful, I would be very grateful if you could spend just five minutes leaving a review (it can be as short as you like) on the book's Amazon page. You can jump right to the page by clicking below:

UK US

  Also, please feel free to email me your thoughts: petecblack@gmail.com

Thank you so much!
  Peter Black

I am on Facebook – https://www. facebook.com/peterblackwriter
I am on Twitter - @petecblack
Please check out my website – www.petercblack.co.uk

CAN THESE OTHER BOOKS HELP?

"Cool That Volcano: How to Help Children Stay Calm, Manage Anger and Master Emotions"

By

Peter Black

Are your children difficult to control? Are you starting to worry that their constant temper tantrums and explosive anger are getting out of hand? You're not alone.

It is a fact that many children experience difficulties in managing their emotions, and can express anger in a damaging way that causes problems for them, and others around them. This book is packed full of techniques and methods that take you through a step by step approach to teaching your children how to manage their emotions, in a concise and easy to read manner. This is not a 300 page technical manual, but it is a set of practical methods which help you to help your child stay in control of, and master their emotions. This will almost certainly improve their lives, and the lives of those who care about them.

In this guide you'll learn how to:

- Teach your child to recognise problematic emotions
- Teach your child how to calm down and manage anger
- Teach your child how to talk about their feelings
- Teach your child how to achieve mastery of their emotions
- Think about your own approach to emotional management
- What are you waiting for? Read this book, apply the methods inside, and begin to improve your child's life today.

Get the book here – https://books2read.com/u/mdlaBd

Printed in Great Britain
by Amazon